How-to-Draw Anything with Just Pencil and Paper

Erik Kopp

ISBN-13: 9781723932953

CONTENTS

INTRODUCTION 3

STAGE 1: GETTING STARTED 4

   Step 1 Have the Right Tools 4

   Step 2 Holding the Pencil 7

   Step 3 Using a Grid 8

   Step 4 BLIND CONTOUR 9

   Step 5 CONTOUR DRAWING 11

STAGE 2: TONE AND SHADING 11

   Step 1 Introduction to Pencil Shading 11

   Step 2 Continuous Shading 13

   Step 3 Realistic Shading 14

STAGE 3: PORTRAIT DRAWING 16

   Step 1 Drawing the Head and Neck 16

   Step 2 How to draw the Eyes and Nose 17

   Step 3 How to draw the Mouth and Ears 21

   Step 4 How to draw Hair 24

   Step 5 Achieving Likeness 25

INTRODUCTION

How-to-Draw with Pencils for Beginners is a practical eBook intended for first-time artists who have a desire to draw but have no experience (novice), for individuals who love to draw but have had no formal training (intermediate) and for the ones who are new students of art (junior).

This eBook will not make you a Michelangelo or Leonardo da Vinci (two of the most famous painters and sculptors of all time), but it will give you a practical step-by-step method to develop the art of drawing with pencils. In order to become a skilled artist, just like learning to play the guitar or the piano, it takes practice.

By following the three stages suggested in this eBook, a series of exercises will challenge you as you follow each step to increase your drawing skills and become a better artist. You will learn how to draw a human face by practicing contour, shaping, shading, and dimensional (realistic) drawing. You cannot afford to skip any steps. You cannot learn everything over night. You will need to do these exercises repeatedly and read this eBook more than one time.

Get ready for an exciting time as you learn ***How-to-Draw with Pencils for Beginners***. Let us get started.

STAGE 1: GETTING STARTED

Step 1 Have the Right Tools

To become an artist, just like a mechanic who works on cars, you have to invest in the *right tools*. Without them, your drawing experience will be more difficult, frustrating and tempt you to quit before you master your skill. A simple trip to your nearest art and craft store is where you will find everything listed in step one.

Pencil

It begins with a *pencil*. Most artists have different preferences for what type of pencil they prefer. Some like mechanical pencils while others choose Progresso pencils (2B and 6B), wood-cased pencils, or graphite lead (6B, 4B, 2B). Each of these pencils has advantages and disadvantages. Some of them are uncomfortable to grip. Some need to be sharpened more often. Some are more fragile and the lead breaks more often. Some have limitations on shading and so on.

As a beginner, you do not want to use the typical pencil you use in school (No. 2), but rather a wood-cased graphite pencil, which is made specifically for shading and sketching.

When it comes to drawing faces, your pencil will act as a brush that can give you fine lines, smooth looks, powered shades, deep impressions and precise strokes. Keeping your pencil sharp is necessary when drawing eyelashes and the lips. Other times, you will want a dull point when shading the cheeks or making waves in the hair.

Over time, you will find your favorite type and brand of pencil that

works best for you.
Pencil Sharpeners

If you select either the Progresso or wood-cased pencils, you will need a *pencil sharpener*. It does not have to be anything fancy. A simple two-hole metal blade pencil sharpener will do just fine. However, it does take a little practice to use. At the wrong angle, you can easily break the lead tip, and before you know it, your pencil is getting smaller and smaller, much quicker than you desire. You will also want to keep a trashcan nearby to discard the shavings.

If you are like many young artists, who recently got started with drawing, you will want to carry your artwork and supplies with you. In this case, you might want to purchase canister pencil sharpener. It is capable of producing fine, needle-sharp points and at the same time, constrain your loose shavings with no mess.

If you do not like to sharpen your pencil by hand, you can use an electric sharpener. However, if you do, you will not be able to see your pencil and have the tendency to over sharpen and shred more than what is necessary. You might be buying more pencils.
Sandpaper

Another helpful tool to keep your pencil sharp is fine *sandpaper*. When drawing the hair, you are covering a larger surface, your pencil will dull easily, and more often, yet find that only the point is dull. This is when the sandpaper comes in handy.

Very fine sandpaper is also useful to clean effectively a tortillon (a tightly wrapped paper blending stump).
Tortillon Blending Tools

A *tortillon* is a tight spiral stick of fibrous paper that is a useful tool when it comes to smudging and blending. You do not want to use your fingers because the oil from your skin or dirt will smear onto your paper and make it difficult to redraw over top of it or erase, and possibly damage the paper.

Kneaded Erasers

Kneaded erasers are very useful for erasing all kinds of areas. Sometimes, while drawing, the sides and palm of your hand attract the lead and it is easy to smudge your portrait accidentally. If the tortillon surface gets dirty, you can pull and fold it to a clean surface. Use a larger piece for large areas, or reshape the flexible material into a point and apply with a twist to erase small spots.

Another option many artists insist upon using is a product called, *Blue Tack*. It too is flexible and can lift the darkest shades (6B) to the lightest shade, which is often necessary when drawing hair or the shading the forehead. It is a great tool when you feel you have over shaded or your tones are too dark.

White Plastic Erasers

A good quality *white plastic eraser* is another useful tool for erasing light areas (the nose or ears) or highlights (hair). Do not buy just any erasers. Avoid less expensive ones because they crumble easy and the material is hard, which makes it more likely to tear your paper when using it. When the edges get dirty, do not attempt to wash them with soap and water or rub with a damp towel. Instead, carefully trim the edge with a knife.

Sketchbook

Whether you are a beginner or been drawing for a while, you will want to purchase a good quality *sketchbook*. There are many options to choose from at Michael's or your favorite art and craft store. A favorite is the *Mead Academie Sketch Portfolio*, which is very inexpensive (around $8) and can be purchased at any Office Max or at Amazon.com.

Sketchbooks come in different sizes (11" x 8.5" or larger) with 50-70 sheets and the paper thickness is just right. You will want to select a paper grade that is 60 pound. The label will tell you what the paper thickness is for each sketchpad.

Your sketchbook will become your artistic journal and has many advantages. It is an easy way to keep your drawings safe and all together in one location. Spiral sketchbooks allow you to remove individual sheets for framing and gifts to family and friends. It is also a good way to map your success, showing your progression as an artist.

Step 2 Holding the Pencil

There are many opinions as how an artist should *hold a pencil*. At times, you may draw for two hours or more, and holding a pencil improperly will cause unnecessary strain on your fingers and cramps in your forearm. Without the proper grip, you will find it difficult to make the right shade or will press too hard or too soft when drawing your lines and contours.

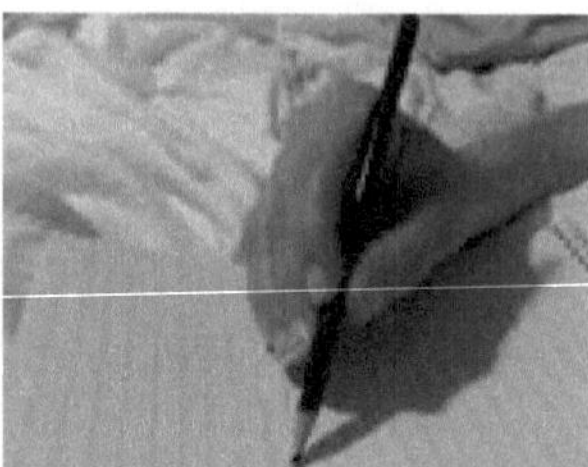

The suggested method to hold a pencil for drawing is the *tripod grip*. It is called this because you use three fingers—your thumb, index and middle finger to secure the pencil, using your ring and pinky fingers to position your hand at the proper distance from the paper. Holding the pencil at a slight angle in an upright position allows for accurate shading and drawing lines with the tip, rather than the side of the pencil lead.

Step 3 Using a Grid

Nothing can frustrate a novice more than to feel like your drawings are poorly done because the shapes and sizes are out of proportion. Many times, you can get irritated and tempted to quit. There is a simple exercise that can help you—*grid drawing*. Using a grid is a popular way for beginners to start out. Before you can start drawing faces, you will have to learn how to make contour (shapes) and see depth perspective (3-D, or realistic). To accomplish this, you will want to begin with grid drawing. It is a sure what to begin so that your proportions and layout in a drawing are correct.

When it comes to grid drawing, a few tips are important so that you can obtain the best results without working too hard. It is a very useful exercise where accuracy is important.

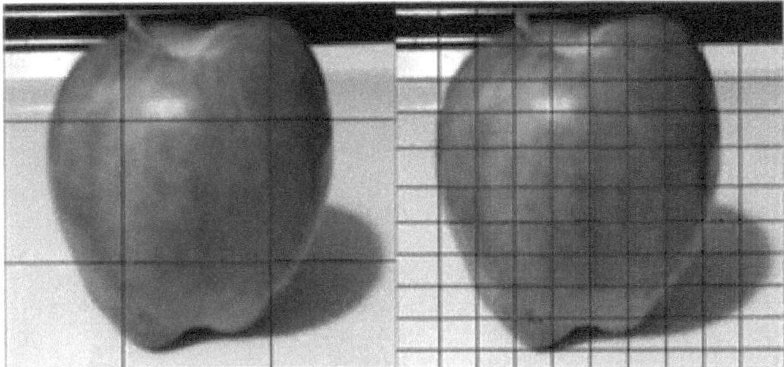

When you choose a picture to draw, make sure it is large and clear. You can photocopy or print a computer image rather than drawing directly on a photograph. You need to make clear lines and not make the grid too large or too small. If it is too large, you might find it difficult to match. If it is too small, it will be difficult to erase. Your lines should be one-inch to a half-inch in size to ensure your drawing comes out right.

Step 4 BLIND CONTOUR

Another exercise that will help you with eye-hand coordination is *blind contour* drawing. It is fun, simple, and an exercise that most all art teachers use. Contour drawing is where you draw only the outline of an object. Blind contour drawing means you draw the outline of the subject without looking at the paper. Your drawing will not look like a masterpiece, but it does not matter. The object is to stare at your object, study its shape and attempt to mimic its proportion.

Now when doing a blind contour drawing, you do not lift the pencil off the paper. You make one continuous line, beginning at the bottom and working your way back to where you started. NO CHEATING! Keep your eyes focused on your object and DO NOT look at your drawing until you are finished.

This would be a good time to try it. Take out your pencil and sketchbook, or a piece of paper. (You might need to tape your paper to a surface to prevent it from sliding). Now, try to draw the opposite hand you draw with. Place it in front of you, a short distance away from your paper. Now, start drawing your hand. Now, concentrate and attempt to draw each detail the best you can. When you are finished, it will probably look something like this:

Looks funny, does it not? Over time, you will get better and remember, this exercise is to develop your eye-hand coordination, not draw a perfect image.

Doing this exercise as many times as you can, and the more you do it, the better it will become. Learning to focus and moving your hand with what you see is important. The better you concentrate the faster you will get and create drawings that are more accurate. Eventually, you will draw something like this:

Step 5 CONTOUR DRAWING

Contour drawing is a simple exercise that develops your skills in shaping an object in proper proportion. The line you draw visibly illustrates the edges of an object. The drawing details such as color, shadows and highlights are not applied in "pure" contour drawing. You only draw clearly defined edges, ignoring the desire to color or add shadows.

STAGE 2: TONE AND SHADING

Now that you have the right tools, have practiced the grid, blind contour, and contour drawing exercises, you are ready to move to the next step, *tone and shading*. If you have not completed these exercises, stop now and go back before you go any further. Mastering these simple tasks is crucial for any artist, no matter how silly they seem.

Step 1 Introduction to Pencil Shading

The next step after contour drawing is *pencil shading*. Shading adds depth and tone to your drawing, especially with portraits. The challenge in drawing with pencil is to make a "colored" picture look realistic with grayscale. Shading enables you to bring texture to the cheeks, eyes, nose and hair.

When it comes to shading, you will need to hold your pencil at a different angle, which might mean you will slightly change your grip. You do not want to use the point of the pencil, but the side of the lead.

This allows you to add tone and not draw a straight line. Lines are used at times when drawing a face, but to create a certain affect, the artist does them on purpose.

However, if you want to draw a portrait and make it realistic, you do not want to use lines, but tone shades. You will want to use short and light strokes, gradually shading. The depth of your shade will depend upon the pressure you add to your pencil.

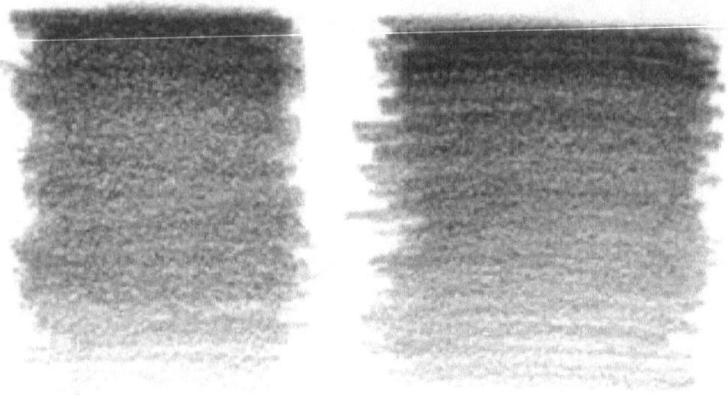

The sample above shows two methods of shading. The one on the left is with the pencil at an angle and the one of the right is with the point. Using the side of the lead allows you to blend and you use this method when you want to demonstrate depth, tone and contrast (cheeks or lips). A sharp point is used when you want to show texture (hair).

Let us start with a simple exercise that will give you the opportunity to practice shading. Using the example above, start at the top and working your way downward, begin shading with pressure and gradually lighten your pencil to make lighter shades. First, use the side of the lead, making a one to two inch box. Second, use the point of your pencil, shading the same size box as the other.

When shading, it is important to keep your pencil sharp, whether you use the point or the side.

Step 2 Continuous Shading

Now, let us go to the next step, *continuous shading*. This exercise is an expansion of step 1. If you were to take a photograph and increase the size, by say, 1200%, you will find that it is made up of a series of boxes, each with a color tone. These boxes are so small, they cannot be seen by the naked eye. Using this method, you will begin to understand the makeup of tone and shading.

Using the sample above, make five grid boxes one-inch square on a piece of paper in your sketchbook. Starting from left to right, shade each box, beginning with dark and gradually go lighter. If you have purchased more than one pencil, try this with different grades, ranging from 6B to 2H. This way can see what each pencil provides in tone and shading.

Once you have completed the five grid boxes, using the sample above, try doing a seven grid grayscale. This time, from left to right, start with a light shade and gradually go darker. Once you complete this exercise, do it again, only this time, start with the darkest shade and gradually go lighter. You will find that different pencils provide lighter and darker shades, so experiment with your shading with a variety of pencils until you find the one that works best for you.

If you have trouble with getting a solid dark shade, the paper grade might be too low. Most copy or computer paper ranges from five pound to twenty pound, which is not recommended for drawing. Remember to purchase 60 pound paper for best results.

Once you have completed the five grid and seven grid shading exercise, now you can practice doing a gradual shade from dark to light without any boxes. Again, use different pencils to see what works best. Make notations in your sketchbook for what pencils work for dark and for light shading. This way, when you are working on drawing objects or portraits in the future, you will know which one to use for the best results. Also, do not use your finger for blending your tones. Instead, use a tortillon. If you have more than one size, use different tortillons for practice. You find that blending your shades with tortillons will smooth the lines and create a desired texture.

Step 3 Realistic Shading

Now that you have completed the shading exercises, it is time to draw an object and practice your shading skills. This is called *realistic shading*. The purpose is to assist you in making light and dark tones according to the light cast upon the object.

When you practiced contour drawing, you only drew a line with no filling. Now it is time to fill the object with shades, which will bring your drawing to life and look realistic. Shading your object brings contours into a three-dimensional shape, showing shadows, points of emphasis that make the object pop off the paper. It brings depth and allows you to leave the line drawing and enter a new realm of art.

You will begin with contour drawing, lightly sketching your lines to create boundaries and shape. Then, after formulating the shape, you begin to add tone with shading and then blending the various tones with your tortillon. Normally, the darkest area is on the border of the shadow side of your object, depending upon the light angle. Begin with the dark areas first, and then shade the lighter areas second.

Be patient with your tone shading. If you get it too dark, no worries, you can use the Blue Tack or a kneaded eraser to remove excess pencil shades. Pay close attention to your object. This is where your eye-hand coordination comes in to play. Look at your object for a few seconds, then look at your paper and draw the specific area you are viewing and repeat. Your goal is to build contrast.

For this exercise, retrieve an egg from the refrigerator, with permission, of course—preferably a white one. If you do not have access to an egg, you can use fruit, an apple or a pear. For this exercise, use a soft 6B pencil, if you have one. It will provide a grainy shaded look. If you prefer a finer, more realistic surface, use a 2B pencil, which will give you more control over the tone, and will shade the paper more evenly.

STAGE 3: PORTRAIT DRAWING

Step 1 Drawing the Head and Neck

Now it is time to begin drawing your portrait. In order to sketch the human head accurately, you first need to become familiar with the basic proportions. A picture of the skull is a good way to study the bone structure of the face. Before you can accurately draw the muscle tone of the cheeks and the arch of the eyebrow, you need to know what is underneath all that skin. Using a skeleton image will help you gain a clear view of the relationship between the skull and the visible surface of the head. The skull shapes the face.

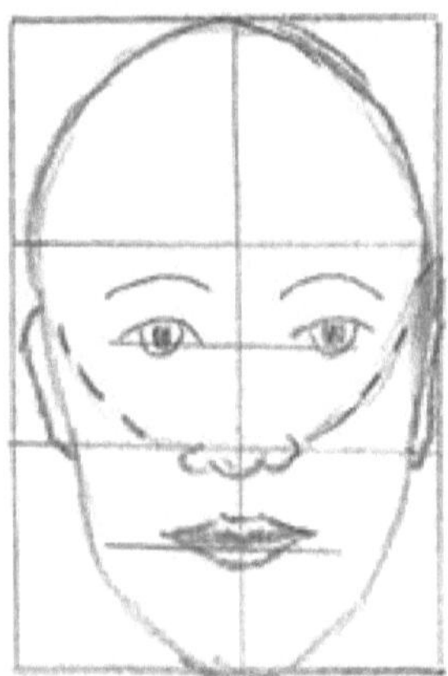

A simple method is to divide the face into six equal squares, two by three. Begin by making a rectangular box. Divide the rectangle in half by drawing a straight line from the top to the bottom. Next, draw two horizontal lines, dividing the rectangle into thirds, as seen here. Next, draw a partial line in the bottom two squares, half the distance. Now, draw a circle in the top four squares. Draw your left and right cheekbones and chin.

Add the eyebrows, eyes, nose and lips.

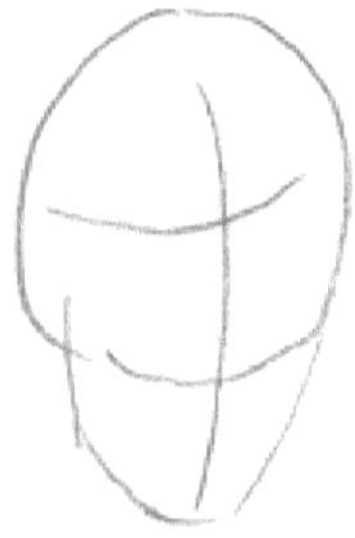

To construct a well-proportioned head, follow these simple steps:

1. Begin with a ball. Make two curved lines, one horizontal and one perpendicular.
2. At the bottom of your ball, starting on the right side, draw an upside down pear. Next, continue the perpendicular line down to the bottom of the chin area.
3. Construct the eyebrows by drawing across the top horizontal line. Next, sketch the nose, using the perpendicular line and the bottom horizontal line. Insert the mouth and reshape the chin position slightly. (The distance from chin to crown is almost the same as from forehead to the back of the skull).

Do this exercise several times in your sketchbook. Each time you do it, you will improve with greater accuracy and proportion. Practice, practice and more practice.

Step 2 How to draw the Eyes and Nose

In this exercise, we must zero in on the anatomy of the eye and uncover some useful tips for getting the eyes with the right size and location. As was true for the skeleton structure of the head, learning what is under the tissue of an eye, you will know what to look for when you are drawing the pupils, and will obtain realistic results in your portrait drawings.

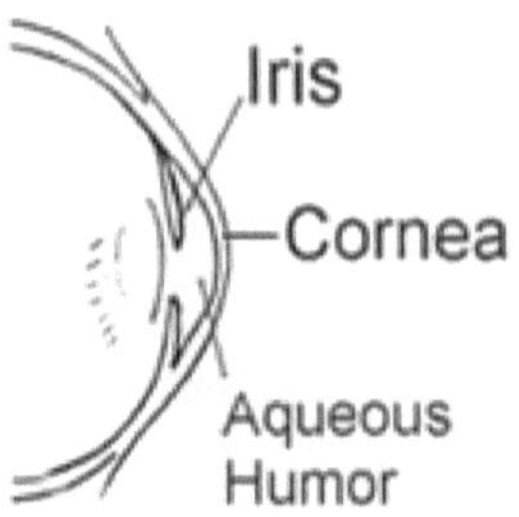

Let us take a quick look at the anatomy of the eye. Now, take a mirror and hold it up to your face. Watch your eyes as they look from side to side. Next, get a friend or a family member to pose for you. Look closely at the eye from a side view. Can you see that the eyeball is not a perfect sphere? The cornea bulges out in front of the iris (the colored part), so that the while the iris looks flat, reflections from the front of the eye show a curved surface. When drawing an eye, it changes position in the socket and makes the shape of the eyelid change slightly.

How you draw the eye also depends on the angle of your subject's head. If they are not looking directly at you, at an angle or three-quarter view, the eyes will also be at an angle. This is a 3-D perspective.

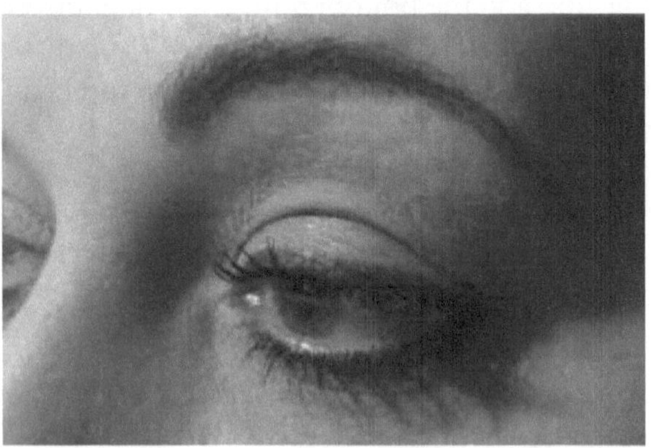

Now it is time try to draw an eye. Use a friend as a model, or look into a mirror and sketch your own. When drawing eyes, focus on a reference point, look in to a certain part of the eye, and begin there. Maybe it is the pupil, eyelid or eyeball. Just start drawing. Remember, start with the contour drawing first, and then go to shaping and shading second.

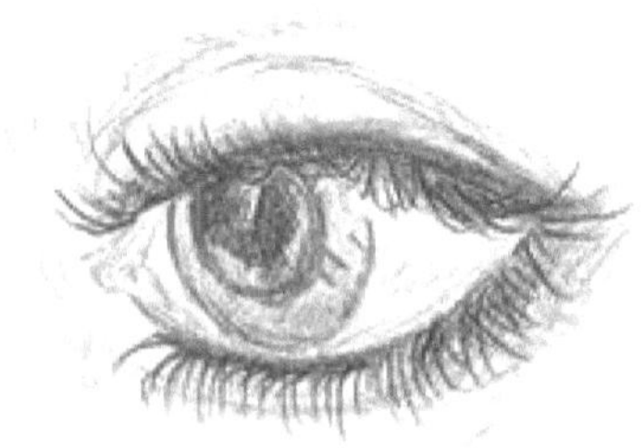

There is a saying that says, "Opinions are like noses, everyone has one." This is true, but not everyone has the same shape. Nose shapes vary immensely from person to person, because of their bone and cartilage structure, as well as the muscles of their face and the amount of fatty tissue under their skin. It is important to observe each person carefully. Before you start drawing, take your time and study your model's (or image) nose. How wide Is It in comparison to the face? How long is it? Are the nostrils small, wide or tight?

When you are drawing people, it helps to know the bone structure of the nose. You do not need to remember the funny names, just so long as you remember roughly what goes where and what it looks like.

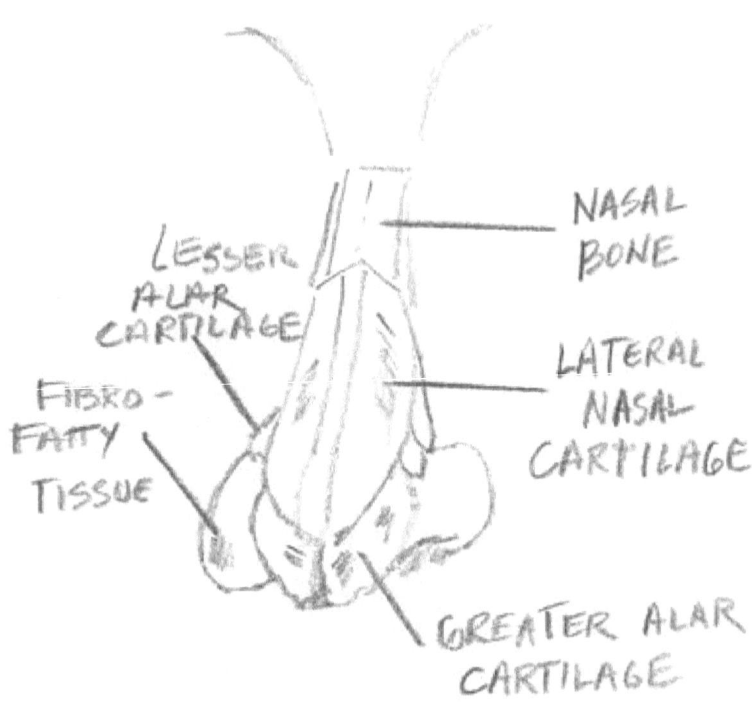

NASAL BONE
LATERAL NASAL CARTILAGE
GREATER ALAR CARTILAGE
LESSER ALAR CARTILAGE
FIBRO-FATTY TISSUE

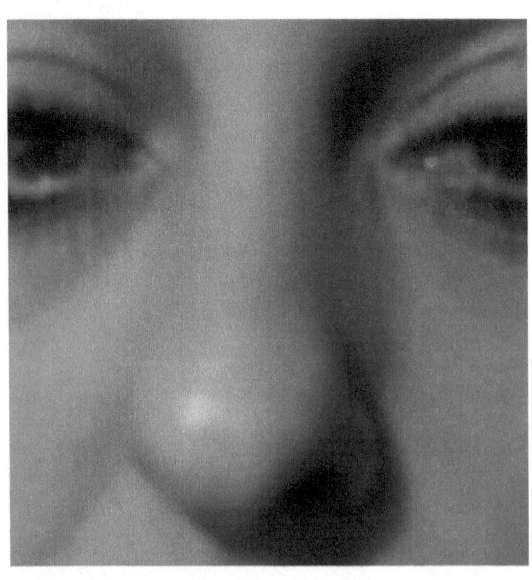

Step 3 How to draw the Mouth and Ears

Again, when drawing any object or image, you need to pay special attention to details. In this 3/4 view, you can clearly see the effect of the curve of the lips, on the right of the photo the line of the mouth is almost parallel to the picture plane, while on the left it drops away. The amount of curve is dependent upon the bone structure and the size and shape of the teeth.

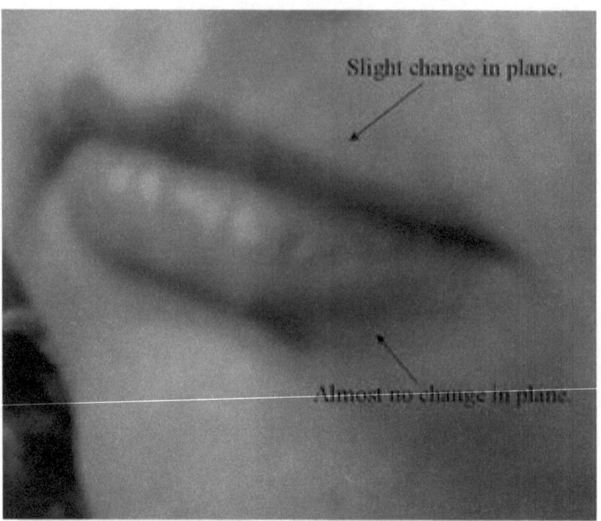

On the bottom lip, you can see that there is very little change of plane between the edges of the mouth and the skin. The lower lip curves gradually. There is a slight crease below the lip, where the shadow drops off, before the outward curve of the chin catches the light.

Here is a simple sketch of the lips pictured. Can you notice something on the lower lip? Look closer again at the photograph and then the drawing. The subject has chapped lips. This is part of observation. Notice the details. It makes it more realistic.

Now, let us move on to drawing an ear. A simple way to shape an ear is to compare it to a heart. If you can imagine a heart shape, then half of this heart shape corresponds to the shape of the ear. Lightly put this shape in with your pencil. It does not need to be perfect at this time, because you can shape it more as you go. Now to add other shapes inside the ear, the inner line this follows the contour of the outer outline.

Pick out the hollow circular shape inside the centre of the ear keeping aware of the distance from the top and bottom of the ear. You can get on with the shading now and carefully observe what is going on in and around the ear like the highlights which are left as white paper and the intricate little shadows, which describe the shapes of the ear.

A simple formula to use for toning and shading the ear, divide it into three areas:

1. Areas that are mostly light, leave these areas unshaded. You can allow your white paper to create a light area.
2. Areas that are mostly dark, shade these areas with a mid-tone. This is where your tortillon will come in handy.
3. Areas that are extremely dark, shade these areas with a darker tone pencil.

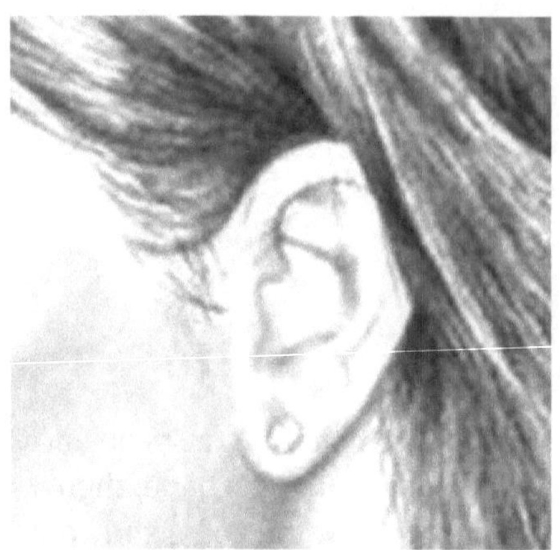

Step 4 How to draw Hair

Hair comes in many shapes, sizes, twists, turns and colors. When you start sketching hair, you need to draw in the direction the hair grows. No matter if the hair is long or short. You need to observe the hairline, hair texture and the direction of growth. Once you figure out which way the hair is growing stay with that flow. Otherwise, the hair will look unnatural.

When drawing short hair, first ensure that the skull is accurately drawn and in proportion, with the ears properly placed. Begin with dark areas first. Then follow the flow toward the lightest areas. When drawing dark to light, always start by pressing hard on the paper and gradually releasing the pressure to where the stroke ends with just a whisper.

Step 5 Achieving Likeness

When you are drawing a portrait, tiny differences can really change the way the face looks. Remember what we have learned. Check the little things, like the way the line at the corner of the mouth tips down, the length of a dimple, the shape of the wrinkles near the eyes. These details make your drawing pop and appear more realistic.

Use a photo taken in natural light, or without flash. The flash floods the face with flat light and it distorts the tones and makes red eyes. If you are using a photograph, try tracing some points to give you guide-points of reference. This is not cheating. For beginners, this is just a tool to help you get started.

Imagine a line straight down the person's face, through the pupil. Does the corner of the lip sit to the left or the right of it? Are the tilt of the eyes is correct? Is the nose wide or long enough? Are the lips the right thickness? Is the jaw line round or square? Is the hairline the right height above the eyes? How thick or thin are the eyebrows?

Pay attention to the hair. Hair tells us a lot about a person and can really change how someone looks. Drawing hair is a difficult task for most beginners. The drawing exercises you have learned will help you to draw hair that looks three-dimensional and shiny.

As a beginner who is just starting out on your drawing journey, try drawing a face of someone who is very close to you. That person could be anyone, a dear friend, a relative, a girlfriend or boyfriend, a person you respect, an athlete or a superstar, a person you have lost. Picking one of these individuals will give you excitement, zeal and anticipation to complete your portrait.

Let us review our steps. Start by drawing the outline of the head. If you are unable to do this freehand, draw a grid to help calculate where each feature stands in relation to the other features. Remember the six grid boxes. The eyes should be on the same line as the top of the ears, the nose, somewhere along the invisible line that joins the middle part of the ears, and the mouth, just below the point where the neck meets the ears.

You should immediately start working on the eyes. You do not have to finish them. Just make sure that you shade the eyes to the point where you feel like your portrait is staring back at you. Do not let the nose sink below the midline of the ears.

Use your tools and shade the areas of the forehead, cheeks, chin and lips. Finally, begin stroking the hair with the grain it grows. Use your tortillon to shade the strokes and strands. For dark areas, press hard and light areas, leave them alone.

Finally, when you are completed, lightly spray your drawing with hairspray to seal the lead.

Following these three stages, you will someday draw a realistic portrait like this:

www.ingramcontent.com/pod-product-compliance
Lightning Source LLC
Chambersburg PA
CBHW051240250726
48656CB00003B/1051